Bible Study Series
for junior high/middle school

THE TRUTH ABOUT

Sin and Forgiveness

Group

Loveland, Colorado

The Truth About Sin and Forgiveness

Core Belief Bible Study Series

Credits

Editor: Karl Leuthauser
Creative Development Editor: Paul Woods
Chief Creative Officer: Joani Schultz
Copy Editor: Janis Sampson
Art Directors: Bill Fisher and Ray Tollison
Cover Art Director: Jeff A. Storm
Computer Graphic Artist: Ray Tollison
Cover Photographer: Jafe Parsons
Production Manager: Gingar Kunkel

ISBN 0-7644-0863-1
10 9 8 7 6 5 4 3 2   06 05 04 03 02 01 00 99

Printed in the United States of America.

Visit our Web site: www.grouppublishing.com

Bible Study Series
for junior high/middle school

contents:

the Core Belief: ▼Sin and Forgiveness

To many of today's young people, "sin" is an outdated word. They have no understanding of absolute right or wrong because the culture around them has obscured these ideas. But absolutes remain—regardless of popular belief. Sin does exist, and that's why today's young people need to learn the lessons within this Core Christian Belief.

Sin is falling short of God's standard of perfection. Since the day Adam and Eve sinned by eating forbidden fruit, each of us has separated ourselves from God. We doom ourselves to physical and spiritual death by our disobedience. But God has bridged that gap through the death and resurrection of his Son, Jesus Christ. Because of this, God can forgive us and restore us to a relationship with him. We still sin, and he still forgives. And because he's forgiven us, he wants us to forgive others too.

the ▼Helpful Stuff

the ▼Studies

studies

▼Sin and Forgiveness
as a Core Christian Belief

Kids today have been desensitized to sin. They're bombarded by all manner of sin in movies and television. Violence and killing are "fun" and acceptable. Sex outside of marriage is exciting and attractive—and often displayed in graphic explicitness. Ethics in business—or in daily life—are only for the weak or naive. Crime is profitable and reasonable—if you're smart enough to get away with it. And anyone standing up for Christian values or pure living comes off looking like a fool.

To young people, sin and its consequences can seem unreal—like a used-up idea that's lost its merit in the flood of popular opinion. They see no need for God or the forgiveness he offers. Consequently, it shouldn't surprise us that few kids really take God seriously. Nevertheless, God's love for young people remains unchanged.

The first study of *The Truth About Sin and Forgiveness* will help kids shatter the greatest barrier between our plight of sin and the abundance of God's mercy. The study will help your kids see that **pride** is a deadly and devastating sin that separates them from the forgiveness and assurance they desperately need.

The second study will remind your students that God's forgiveness is complete. You'll show them that the work Jesus did on the cross gives them the opportunity to let go of **guilt**—whether it's from things they've done or what has been done to them.

In the third study, you'll explain that forgiveness follows **repentance.** Kids will be challenged to turn to God as you help them understand that admitting they're wrong helps them change their ways.

The final study of *The Truth About Sin and Forgiveness* will teach your kids to stop sin before it starts. By looking at **fantasy,** your kids will discover that sin starts in the mind. They'll be encouraged to guard their hearts and minds to prevent the seeds of sin from growing out of control.

Understanding the effects and reality of sin can help your kids see their need for God's forgiveness. Only then can they appreciate the cost Jesus paid to allow them the chance to know God and walk with him.

*For a more comprehensive look at this Core Christian Belief, read Group's **Get Real: Making Core Christian Beliefs Relevant to Teenagers.***

DEPTH FINDER

HOW THE BIBLE DESCRIBES SIN AND FORGIVENESS

To help you effectively guide your kids toward this Core Christian Belief, use these overviews as a launching point for a more in-depth study of sin and forgiveness.

- **Sin is essentially falling short of what God wants us to do.** We sin by doing things that don't please God, and we sin by not doing things that God wants us to do. Some picture it as missing the mark, like when you shoot an arrow at a target and don't hit it. Sin happens when we place ourselves above God by choosing to do what we want instead of what God wants (Deuteronomy 25:16; Ephesians 2:1-3; James 1:14-15; 4:17; 1 John 3:4; 5:17).

- **Adam and Eve introduced sin to humanity.** The sin they committed involved direct disobedience to one of God's commands. Prior to their sin, they didn't have the sinful nature we have. They were tempted by an outside source—the serpent, who was really Satan—and when they gave in to the temptation, sin permanently entered the human race. They chose to believe and obey the serpent rather than God, and all humans have been plagued by sin since that day (Genesis 3:1-13; Jeremiah 17:9; John 8:44; Romans 5:12; 1 Corinthians 15:21-22).

- **All people in every age have sinned.** Because of the sin nature introduced by Adam and Eve, without God's help no human is able to refrain from sinning (1 Kings 8:46; Job 14:4; Ecclesiastes 7:20; Isaiah 53:6; Romans 3:10-12, 23; 1 John 1:8).

- **Sin causes both physical and spiritual death.** God's standard is perfection, and with one single sin we've lost all possibility of being perfect. Therefore, we're cut off from God, and destined for spiritual and physical destruction. There's nothing we can do to wipe out our own sin and make ourselves good enough to have a relationship with God. We're totally at his mercy (Genesis 2:17; Isaiah 57:20-21; 59:2; Matthew 5:48; Romans 6:23; Galatians 6:7-8).

- **God is ready to forgive *anyone* who seeks him.** Because of Jesus' death and resurrection, God can forgive our sins, and restore our relationship with him. To receive God's forgiveness, we must confess our sin to him and turn away from the sin. When possible, we should make restitution for any wrong we've done against others. We must also be willing to forgive others who've wronged us if we want God to forgive us (Psalm 103:1-3; Matthew 5:23-24; 18:23-35; Luke 15:11-24; Colossians 1:13-14; 1 John 1:9).
- **Though Christians try to please God, they still struggle with sin.** When we sin, we don't forfeit our relationship with God, but our fellowship with him is broken. Fortunately, forgiveness is readily available, and condemnation is nullified through the redeeming work of Jesus Christ in our lives (Romans 7:15-25; 8:1-2; Galatians 5:13-26; Ephesians 4:17–5:20; 1 John 1:9).
- **God commands us to forgive others in the same way he has forgiven us.** God has made it clear that we're not to condemn others, or seek revenge for the wrongs others commit. Instead, we're to turn the other cheek and forgive when we're wronged (Matthew 5:39; 18:21-22; Luke 17:3-4; Ephesians 4:32; Colossians 3:13).

CORE CHRISTIAN BELIEF OVERVIEW

Here are the twenty-four Core Christian Belief categories that form the backbone of Core Belief Bible Study Series:

The Nature of God	Jesus Christ	The Holy Spirit
Humanity	Evil	Suffering
Creation	The Spiritual Realm	The Bible
Salvation	Spiritual Growth	Personal Character
God's Justice	Sin & Forgiveness	The Last Days
Love	The Church	Worship
Authority	Prayer	Family
Service	Relationships	Sharing Faith

Look for Group's Core Belief Bible Study Series books in these other Core Christian Beliefs!

Bible Study Series
for junior high/middle school

Think for a moment about your young people. When your students walk out of your youth program after they graduate from junior high or high school, what do you want them to know? What foundation do you want them to have so they can make wise choices?

You probably want them to know the essentials of the Christian faith. You want them to base everything they do on the foundational truths of Christianity. Are you meeting this goal?

If you have any doubt that your kids will walk into adulthood knowing and living by the tenets of the Christian faith, then you've picked up the right book. All the books in Group's Core Belief Bible Study Series encourage young people to discover the essentials of Christianity and to put those essentials into practice. Let us explain...

What Is Group's Core Belief Bible Study Series?

Group's Core Belief Bible Study Series is a biblically in-depth study series for junior high and senior high teenagers. This Bible study series utilizes four defining commitments to create each study. These "plumb lines" provide structure and continuity for every activity, study, project, and discussion. They are:

● **A Commitment to Biblical Depth**—Core Belief Bible Study Series is founded on the belief that kids not only *can* understand the deeper truths of the Bible but also *want* to understand them. Therefore, the activities and studies in this series strive to explain the "why" behind every truth we explore. That way, kids learn principles, not just rules.

● **A Commitment to Relevance**—Most kids aren't interested in abstract theories or doctrines about the universe. They want to know how to live successfully right now, today, in the heat of problems they can't ignore. Because of this, each study connects a real-life need with biblical principles that speak directly to that need. This study series finally bridges the gap between Bible truths and the real-world issues kids face.

● **A Commitment to Variety**—Today's young people have been raised in a sound bite world. They demand variety. For that reason, no two meetings in this study series are shaped exactly the same.

● **A Commitment to Active and Interactive Learning**—Active learning is learning by doing. Interactive learning simply takes active learning a step further by having kids teach each other what they've learned. It's a process that helps kids internalize and remember their discoveries.

For a more detailed description of these concepts, see the section titled "Why Active and Interactive Learning Works With Teenagers" beginning on page 57.

So how can you accomplish all this in a set of four easy-to-lead Bible studies? By weaving together various "power" elements to produce a fun experience that leaves kids challenged and encouraged.

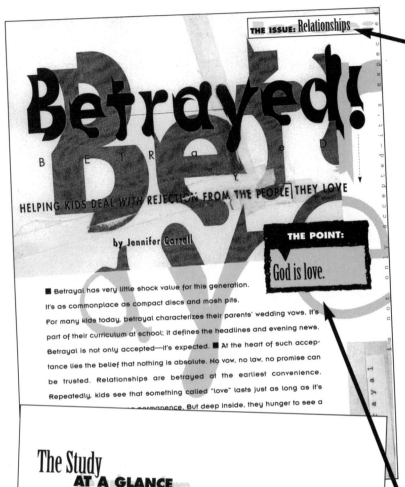

- **A Relevant Topic**—More than ever before, kids live in the now. What matters to them and what attracts their hearts is what's happening in their world at this moment. For this reason, every Core Belief Bible Study focuses on a particular hot topic that kids care about.

- **A Core Christian Belief**—Group's Core Belief Bible Study Series organizes the wealth of Christian truth and experience into twenty-four Core Christian Belief categories. These twenty-four headings act as umbrellas for a collection of detailed beliefs that define Christianity and set it apart from the world and every other religion. Each book in this series features one Core Christian Belief with lessons suited for junior high or senior high students.

  "But," you ask, "won't my kids be bored talking about all these spiritual beliefs?" No way! As a youth leader, you know the value of using hot topics to connect with young people. Ultimately teenagers talk about issues because they're searching for meaning in their lives. They want to find the one equation that will make sense of all the confusing events happening around them. Each Core Belief Bible Study answers that need by connecting a hot topic with a powerful Christian principle. Kids walk away from the study with something more solid than just the shifting ebb and flow of their own opinions. They walk away with a deeper understanding of their Christian faith.

- **The Point**—This simple statement is designed to be the intersection between the Core Christian Belief and the hot topic. Everything in the study ultimately focuses on The Point so that kids study it and allow it time to sink into their hearts.

- **The Study at a Glance**—A quick look at this chart will tell you what kids will do, how long it will take them to do it, and what supplies you'll need to get it done.

• The Bible Connection—This is the power base of each study. Whether it's just one verse or several chapters, The Bible Connection provides the vital link between kids' minds and their hearts. The content of each Core Belief Bible Study reflects the belief that the true power of God—the power to expose, heal, and change kids' lives—is contained in his Word.

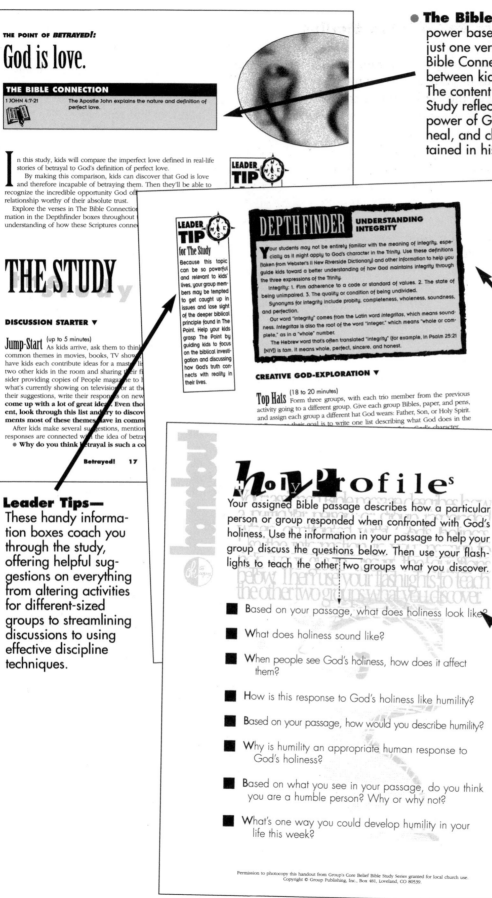

THE POINT OF *BETRAYED!*:

God is love.

THE BIBLE CONNECTION

1 JOHN 4:7-21   The Apostle John explains the nature and definition of perfect love.

In this study, kids will compare the imperfect love defined in real-life stories of betrayal to God's definition of perfect love.

By making this comparison, kids can discover that God is love and therefore incapable of betraying them. Then they'll be able to recognize the incredible opportunity God off...
relationship worthy of their absolute trust.

Explore the verses in The Bible Connection...
mation in the Depthfinder boxes throughout...
understanding of how these Scriptures conne...

THE STUDY

DISCUSSION STARTER ▼

Jump-Start (up to 5 minutes) As kids arrive, ask them to thin...
common themes in movies, books, TV show...
have kids each contribute ideas for a mast...
two other kids in the room and sharing t...
sider providing copies of People magaz...
what's currently showing on televisio...
their suggestions, write their respon...
come up with a lot of great idea...
ent, look through this list and...
ments most of these themes...

After kids make several sugg...
responses are connected w...

• **Why do you think...**

Betrayed!   **17**

LEADER TIP for The Study
Because this topic can be so powerful and relevant to kids' lives, your group members may be tempted to get caught up in issues and lose sight of the deeper biblical principle found in The Point. Help your kids grasp The Point by guiding kids to focus on the biblical investigation and discussing how God's truth connects with reality in their lives.

DEPTHFINDER   UNDERSTANDING INTEGRITY

Your students may not be entirely familiar with the meaning of integrity, especially as it might apply to God's character in the Trinity. Use these definitions (taken from Webster's II New Riverside Dictionary) and other information to help you guide kids toward a better understanding of how God maintains integrity through the three expressions of the Trinity.

Integrity: 1. Firm adherence to a code or standard of values. 2. The state of being unimpaired. 3. The quality or condition of being undivided.

Synonyms for integrity include probity, completeness, wholeness, soundness, and perfection.

Our word "integrity" comes from the Latin word *integritas*, which means soundness. *Integritas* is also the root of the word "integer," which means "whole or complete," as in a "whole" number.

The Hebrew word that's often translated "integrity" (for example, in Psalm 25:21 [NIV]) is *tam*, it means whole, perfect, sincere, and honest.

CREATIVE GOD-EXPLORATION ▼

Top Hats (18 to 20 minutes) Form three groups, with each trio member from the previous activity going to a different group. Give each group Bibles, paper, and pens, and assign each group a different hat God wears: Father, Son, or Holy Spirit.
...their goal is to write one list describing what God does in the...God's character.

• **Depthfinder Boxes**—These informative sidelights located throughout each study add insight into a particular passage, word, historical fact, or Christian doctrine. Depthfinder boxes also provide insight into teen culture, adolescent development, current events, and philosophy.

• **Leader Tips**—These handy information boxes coach you through the study, offering helpful suggestions on everything from altering activities for different-sized groups to streamlining discussions to using effective discipline techniques.

holy Profiles

Your assigned Bible passage describes how a particular person or group responded when confronted with God's holiness. Use the information in your passage to help your group discuss the questions below. Then use your flashlights to teach the other two groups what you discover.

■ Based on your passage, what does holiness look like?

■ What does holiness sound like?

■ When people see God's holiness, how does it affect them?

■ How is this response to God's holiness like humility?

■ Based on your passage, how would you describe humility?

■ Why is humility an appropriate human response to God's holiness?

■ Based on what you see in your passage, do you think you are a humble person? Why or why not?

■ What's one way you could develop humility in your life this week?

• **Handouts**—Most Core Belief Bible Studies include photocopiable handouts to use with your group. Handouts might take the form of a fun game, a lively discussion starter, or a challenging study page for kids to take home—anything to make your study more meaningful and effective.

The Last Word on Core Belief Bible Studies

Soon after you begin to use Group's Core Belief Bible Study Series, you'll see signs of real growth in your group members. Your kids will gain a deeper understanding of the Bible and of their own Christian faith. They'll see more clearly how a relationship with Jesus affects their daily lives. And they'll grow closer to God.

But that's not all. You'll also see kids grow closer to one another.

That's because this series is founded on the principle that Christian faith grows best in the context of relationship. Each study uses a variety of interactive pairs and small groups and always includes discussion questions that promote deeper relationships. The friendships kids will build through this study series will enable them to grow *together* toward a deeper relationship with God.

A LITTLE TOO COOL

Survival Tactics of a Hurting Generation

by Michael D. Warden

■ Hope is a rare commodity for young people these days. ■ Barraged since childhood with the judgments of elder generations, today's teenagers are repeatedly beat down with pronouncements that they're too lazy, too materialistic, too selfish, too bored, or too stupid to warrant any hope for "redemption." ■ In a subtle twist of defiance, teenagers have embraced their elders' judgments with a practiced "yeah, whatever" complacency— not denying their own failings, but choosing instead to wear them like a badge. As a result, this is the first generation for whom hopelessness has become "cool." ■ This study examines kids' hopelessness as a subtle form of pride and explores ways that pride hinders the flow of forgiveness in their lives.

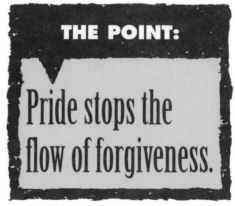

THE POINT:

Pride stops the flow of forgiveness.

The Study
AT A GLANCE

SECTION	MINUTES	WHAT STUDENTS WILL DO	SUPPLIES
Experiential Study	15 to 20	NUMB-FRIENDS LEAGUE—Form two teams to see which can "numbify" one of its members the best.	Toilet paper, tape, paper wads, newsprint, marker, "Life of a Leper" handout (p. 23)
Focused Study	15 to 20	GOING DEEPER—Learn about Naaman in 2 Kings 5 by presenting an "act as you go" skit.	Bibles, index cards, pen, tape or pins, string
	10 to 15	LEPER CONNECTIONS—Talk about how Naaman's story can teach them about sin, pride, and forgiveness.	Bibles
Challenge	5 to 10	CLEANSINGS—Be challenged to wear their "sin" lists until they take private time to talk to God about them.	Index cards, pencils

notes:

THE POINT OF *A LITTLE TOO COOL*:

Pride stops the flow of forgiveness.

THE BIBLE CONNECTION

2 KINGS 5:1-17   Elisha instructs the leper Naaman to wash seven times in the Jordan River so he can be healed.

PROVERBS 3:34   Solomon writes of the relationship between pride, humility, and grace.

I n this study, kids will compare their reactions to brokenness in their lives with Naaman's reaction to his leprosy; then use Naaman's story to examine the connection between sin, pride, forgiveness, and hope.

By understanding Naaman's experience, kids can discover how pride undermines their ability to receive God's forgiveness.

Explore the verses in The Bible Connection, then study the information in the Depthfinder boxes to gain a deeper understanding of how these Scriptures connect with your young people.

LEADER TIP for The Study

Because this topic can be so powerful and relevant to kids' lives, your group members may be tempted to get caught up in issues and lose sight of the deeper biblical principle found in The Point. Help your kids grasp The Point by guiding kids to focus on the biblical investigation and discussing how God's truth connects with reality in their lives.

THE STUDY

EXPERIENTIAL STUDY ▼

Numb-Friends League
(15 to 20 minutes)

After everyone has arrived and settled in, ask:
● **Who can tell me some of the symptoms of leprosy?**

Write kids' responses on newsprint. If necessary, complete the list by looking at the leprosy information in the "Leprosy and Sin" Depthfinder (p. 20). Once the list is complete, say: **Leprosy isn't that common in our country anymore. But this is one disease that the Bible makes** a big deal about. The word "leprosy" or "leper" appears in the Bible over sixty times.

Ask:

● **Why would the Bible use up so much space talking about leprosy?**

Say: **Today our (rather morbid) goal is to answer the question: What can leprosy teach us about real life today?**

Form two teams, and have each team choose one person to act as the "Numb Friend." Say: **Before we can grasp any lessons from leprosy, we need to understand a bit more about what the disease is like.** Explain that both teams' goal is to "numbify" their Numb Friends—that is, to insulate their sense of touch so they can't feel anything touch them.

Set out several rolls of toilet paper and tape, and allow teams to go to work. Warn them that the other team will test their work in five minutes, so they need to work fast and do their best.

After five minutes, call time. Stand both Numb Friends in the front of the room and have them close their eyes. Have teams stand twenty feet away. Give each team member one paper wad, and have kids take turns throwing paper wads at the other team's Numb Friend.

Each time either of the Numb Friends feels a paper wad make contact, have that person raise a hand (or make some other gesture to indicate the hit). The team whose Numb Friend has the fewest "hit sensations" at the end of the game wins.

After the game, allow the Numb Friends to remove their numbing material, then have everyone form a circle. Give a copy of the "Life of a Leper" handout (p. 23) to the Numb Friend from the winning team, and ask him or her to read it aloud.

Say: **As you listen to this letter, think about how you'd feel if you were in Branson's shoes.**

After the reading, ask:

● **What does this letter tell you about leprosy's effect on Branson's life?**

● **How would life change for Branson if doctors discovered a cure for leprosy?**

● **If the cure for leprosy required Branson to soak in hot manure for seven days, do you think he would do it? Why or why not?**

● **If you had leprosy, would you endure the hot-manure cure? Why or why not?**

● **What if your leprosy was hidden and had no outward signs, and you were sure the disease wouldn't show symptoms for years to come. Would you still take the cure? Why or why not?**

Say: **Most likely none of you will ever have to deal with leprosy. But the truth is that all of us suffer from a "disease" that's very much like leprosy in some ways—except this disease attacks the soul instead of the body.**

Through the rest of our time together, we're going to discover that pride stops God's flow of forgiveness, the only cure we have for the disease of sin.

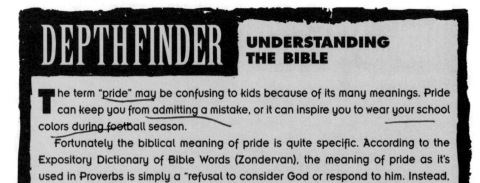

DEPTHFINDER

UNDERSTANDING THE BIBLE

The term "pride" may be confusing to kids because of its many meanings. Pride can keep you from admitting a mistake, or it can inspire you to wear your school colors during football season.

Fortunately the biblical meaning of pride is quite specific. According to the Expository Dictionary of Bible Words (Zondervan), the meaning of pride as it's used in Proverbs is simply a "refusal to consider God or respond to him. Instead, the arrogant supposes that human beings can live successfully apart from an obedient relationship with the Lord."

For more verses on pride, see Proverbs 11:2; 13:10; 16:5; 16:18-19; 18:12; 21:4; and 29:23.

FOCUSED STUDY ▼

Going Deeper

(15 to 20 minutes) Have kids open their Bibles to 2 Kings 5:1-17. Say: **We're going to take a deeper look at someone who needed help from God but found that his pride got in the way. As we look at the Scripture today, let's ask God to help us understand this story and how it applies to us personally.**

Ask a few young people to voice one-sentence prayers, asking God to help them grasp what the passage is trying to teach them. After the prayers, ask kids to read through the passage silently. Then say: **Let's experience this story in a spontaneous way.**

Write each of the following character names on separate index cards, then tape or pin a card to the shirt of each young person.

- Naaman (commander of Aram's army)
- Soldiers
- Young Servant Girl (from Israel)
- Naaman's Wife
- Naaman's Master (King of Aram)
- The Letter (sent from the King of Aram to the King of Israel)
- King of Israel
- Elisha, the Man of God
- Naaman's Horses and Chariots
- Elisha's Messenger
- Naaman's Servants

Explain that someone will read aloud the passage slowly and allow time for the characters to spontaneously act out their parts. Say: **As we act our way through this passage, look for things Naaman does that remind you of your relationship with God.**

If you have a highly dramatic reader in your group, ask him or her to read the passage while you participate in the action. Otherwise, read the passage yourself, making sure to pause frequently so kids can act out their parts. Note: For the skit, use the New International Version of the Bible.

After the skit, give kids a round of applause, and give each a twenty-four-inch section of string as a symbol of the dramatic "string of events" they just dramatized.

LEADER TIP

for Going Deeper

If your group is small, it's OK to give kids multiple character names. If your group is large, you can make all the extra people Soldiers or Naaman's Servants, or you can form two groups and have each perform the passage in turn.

DEPTH FINDER — LEPROSY AND SIN: PROVOKING PARALLELS

LEPROSY ATTACKS THE BODY...

● Leprosy is a slow-growing, chronic infection of the peripheral nervous system. Its initial symptom (often ignored) is numbness in particular areas of the skin.

● With the loss of touch sensation, the body becomes more subject to injury. Without knowing it, a leper can burn, cut, or chafe his or her body with absolutely no sensation of pain.

● For people who have leprosy, the disease becomes the single most dominating factor of their lives.

● When injuries do occur, the natural healing process is hindered because of poor blood circulation to the infected areas. As a result, simple injuries can eventually cause the loss of fingers, toes, nasal tissue, or other parts of the body frequently exposed to the elements.

● Lepers are typically shunned by others.

● As of now, there is still no cure for leprosy.

...AS SIN ATTACKS THE SOUL.

● Sin attacks the soul by slowly "searing" the conscience, taking away its ability to discern right from wrong (1 Timothy 4:1-2). The first sign of this "numbness" (often ignored) is decreased sensitivity to sin.

● With the loss of spiritual sensitivity, the soul becomes more subject to injury. Without realizing it, a person's continued sin can undermine his or her sense of purpose and destroy vital relationships (Ephesians 4:17-19).

● People who continue to sin become enslaved to it (Romans 6:15-23).

● When sinful actions do injure a person's heart, the healing process is hindered or halted altogether because the sin separates the person from God (Isaiah 59:1-2). Hurts that are kept from God will eventually result in complete emotional and spiritual deadness.

● Sin creates a barrier to intimacy between people (Galatians 5:13-15).

● Jesus provided the cure for sin at the cost of his own life (1 Peter 2:24).

[handwritten margin note: Contagious / no cure]

Say: **Naaman's pride almost kept him from getting the help from God that he needed. That same pride can keep us from God, too, if we let it. <u>Pride stops the flow of forgiveness,</u> but with humility comes healing and life.**

Leper Connections (10 to 15 minutes)

Have kids form groups of four. Say: **Let's see what we can learn from Naaman's example.**

In their small groups, have kids discuss each of these questions:

● **What did Naaman do that reminded you of your relationship with God?**

● **Why do you think Naaman was so hesitant to wash in the Jordan, even if it meant being healed of leprosy?**

● **Why do you think we're often so hesitant to go to God or others to ask forgiveness?**

● **Based on the information you've heard today, what can the** effects of leprosy teach us about the effects of sin in our lives?

● **Given all these parallels, why do we still often choose to hang onto sin?**

Have a volunteer in each group read aloud Proverbs 3:34. Then have group members discuss these questions:

● **This passage says that God mocks people who have pride but gives grace to people who are humble. If God really loves us unconditionally, why doesn't he just help us automatically, regardless of our attitude?**

● **What if you don't think something you do is wrong, even though the Bible says it is? What should you do?**

Call everyone together and say: **Pride happens any time you set aside God's authority in your life and follow your own way instead. Our <u>pride stops the flow of God's forgiveness</u> because it can keep us from coming to God for help. Pride has a way of making us believe that we can make it on our own, even though the Bible clearly says that we have no hope outside of Christ** (Ephesians 2:11-13).

Ask:

● **How does your pride keep you from God?**

● **How does your pride keep sin alive in your life?**

"The Lord's curse is on the house of the wicked, but he blesses the home of the righteous. He mocks proud mock-ers but gives grace to the humble."
—Proverbs 3:33-34

CHALLENGE ▼

Cleansings (5 to 10 minutes) Distribute pencils and index cards, then have students write their names at one end of their cards. Under their names, have kids write all the sins they struggle with that they haven't talked to God about recently.

When kids are finished, have each one use the pencil to punch a small hole in the card, then thread the string (from the "Going Deeper" activity) through to make a necklace.

Ask kids to hang their "sin" necklaces around their necks. Then say: **I challenge you not to remove your list of sins until you've taken time to talk with God about each item you wrote. Don't let your <u>pride block the flow of God's forgiveness</u> in your life. Go to him. He's waiting for you.**

Dismiss the class.

Life of a Leper

Dear fellow teenagers,

My name is Branson Reed. I live in a small town not far from Chicago. I'm still in high school, but I spend most of my days studying at home.

I'm supposed to tell you something about my leprosy and how it feels to be a "leper" in America. I'm not sure you'll be able to relate to anything I'm going to say. But maybe you can.

I've had leprosy since I was eight. Nobody knows how I got it, or who I got it from. When that happens, they call it a "primary case." Anyway, after I got it, everybody started treating me differently. My mom, my dad, even my older sister. When the neighborhood families found out, they stopped letting me come over or get around their kids. Eventually I had to drop out of school, and Mom started teaching me at home. I got really depressed a lot as a kid. I couldn't understand why people were so afraid of me.

Now I guess I've gotten used to the way people treat me. I understand it's because of the leprosy and not because of me. Recently I even got into a program that allows me to spend time with other kids in a regular classroom.

I wanted to do it, you know, because things get kind of lonely sometimes. But I got pretty much what I expected. Lots of stares. Everyone keeps their distance. Sometimes I think I'd give anything just to have somebody come up and put an arm around my shoulder or even shake my hand. But that's not gonna happen. And I don't have any feeling in my hands anymore, anyway.

So, what's it like to be a teenage leper? It stinks. I want to yell, "It's not my fault!" But I don't think it would make a difference anymore. Nobody's listening. They all just pretend I don't exist. My greatest fear is that someday I'll believe them and stop trying to live at all.

I guess if I have any "last words," it's this: Don't ignore the outcasts around you. Someday you might be an outcast, too.

All the best,

Branson

According to the World Health Organization, 157 new cases of leprosy were reported in the United States in 1996. The feelings and circumstances of this letter are probable, however the names and events are fictitious.

Feeling Guilty

by Jennifer Root Wilger

The Private Burden Kids Can't Shake

■ Guilt. The word itself can weigh anyone down. The judge pounds the gavel and proclaims the verdict— guilty. And it's off to prison—the prison of the mind where guilt relentlessly haunts and accuses. The feeling of guilt itself can be punishment enough.

■ Your kids walk around with a load of guilt too big for them to bear. And who's the judge that proclaims the guilty verdict? Sometimes it's parents, teachers, and friends who dole out unsolicited evaluations and unwanted comparisons: ■ "Why can't you be more like your sister?" ■ "Can't you get better grades?" ■ "If you'd obeyed your father more, he wouldn't have left us!" ■ Other times your kids truly mess up. They drink, they lie, they steal. This time God wields the gavel, declaring the guilty verdict. Either way you slice it, guilt hurts. It drags people down with a burden they can't overcome alone. ■ This study explores both sides of guilt—the true and the false— to help kids discover that God wants to free them from *all* the guilt they feel.

THE POINT:

God can free you from feelings of guilt.

The Study
AT A GLANCE

SECTION	MINUTES	WHAT STUDENTS WILL DO	SUPPLIES
Preparation	up to 5	ALL ABOARD—Create rules for the guilt trip.	Newsprint, marker, tape, water-based marker
Guilt Trip	10 to 15	STATION 1: ALPHABET GUILT—Display a letter that represents something they feel guilty about.	
	15 to 20	STATION 2: GUILT-O-METERS—Create "machines" to represent false guilt.	Bibles, "Job's True and False Guilt" Depthfinder (p. 30), marbles, sandwich bags, string, masking tape, poster board
	10 to 15	STATION 3: HEART MONITOR—Create a "heart monitor" to indicate how guilty they'd feel if caught in certain situations and discuss the differences between true and false guilt.	Bibles, index cards, pencils, "True or False?" Depthfinder (p. 29), masking tape
Unpacking and Debriefing	5 to 10	WIPE IT OUT—Remove each other's guilt objects.	Bible, clean rags, bowl of soapy water

notes:

God can free you from feelings of guilt.

THE BIBLE CONNECTION

JOB 11:1-20; 12:2-5; 42:1-11

These passages express how Job handled both false and true guilt.

I n this study, kids will explore the differences between "true guilt"—the guilt people feel when they've sinned—and "false guilt"—the "guilt" people feel even if they haven't sinned. Kids will embark on a "Guilt Trip" to collect items representing their guilty feelings and then will have an opportunity to release their true and false guilt.

By taking this trip, kids can discover that God wants to free them from *all* the guilt they feel.

Explore the verses in The Bible Connection, then examine the information in the Depthfinder boxes throughout the study to gain a deeper understanding of how these Scriptures connect with your young people.

BEFORE THE STUDY

Designate a different wall of your meeting room for each station used in this study. Kids will "travel" around your room as they go on their Guilt Trip.

LEADER TIP for The Study

Whenever you tell groups to discuss a list of questions, write the questions on newsprint, and tape the newsprint to the wall so groups can answer the questions at their own pace.

THE STUDY

PREPARATION ▼

LEADER TIP
for All Aboard

Choose commonly used letters such as L, M, R, S, or T for this activity. Students may want to choose their own letters. If they choose rarely-used letters such as Q or Z, you may want to write the letter they choose *and* one of the commonly used letters listed above to make the next activity easier for them.

All Aboard (up to 5 minutes)

After everyone has arrived, say: **Today we're going to look at guilt. To accomplish this, we're going on a Guilt Trip. On our way, we'll explore the differences between false and true guilt and discover that** <u>God can free you from feelings of guilt.</u>

To prepare for the trip, have kids work together to develop at least three "rules for the road" they'll follow as they learn about guilt. For example, some rules might include "Be honest with yourself" or "Don't make fun of others."

Post the rules on newsprint so kids can refer to them throughout the trip. Then say: **We're now ready to embark on our Guilt Trip. To get started, come to the front of the room, and I'll write a letter on your hand.**

As kids come to the front, write a letter of the alphabet on each person's palm with a water-based marker. If you have more than twenty kids, have a volunteer help you with this. Then have kids proceed to Station 1.

"Have mercy on me, **O God,** according to your unfailing *love;* according to your great compassion blot out my transgressions. Wash away all my iniquity and cleanse me from my sin."

—Psalm 51:1-2

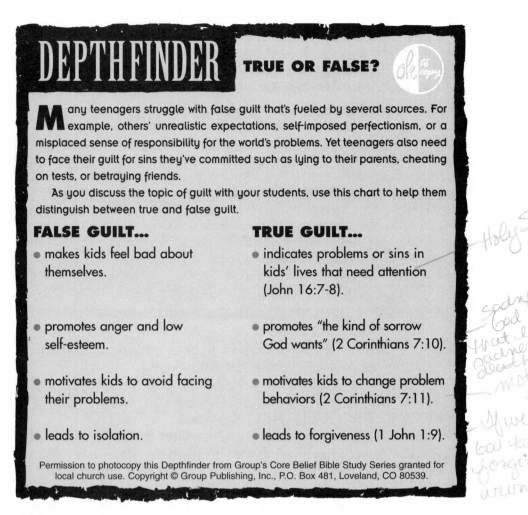

DEPTHFINDER

TRUE OR FALSE?

Many teenagers struggle with false guilt that's fueled by several sources. For example, others' unrealistic expectations, self-imposed perfectionism, or a misplaced sense of responsibility for the world's problems. Yet teenagers also need to face their guilt for sins they've committed such as lying to their parents, cheating on tests, or betraying friends.

As you discuss the topic of guilt with your students, use this chart to help them distinguish between true and false guilt.

FALSE GUILT...

- makes kids feel bad about themselves.

- promotes anger and low self-esteem.

- motivates kids to avoid facing their problems.

- leads to isolation.

TRUE GUILT...

- indicates problems or sins in kids' lives that need attention (John 16:7-8).

- promotes "the kind of sorrow God wants" (2 Corinthians 7:10).

- motivates kids to change problem behaviors (2 Corinthians 7:11).

- leads to forgiveness (1 John 1:9).

Permission to photocopy this Depthfinder from Group's Core Belief Bible Study Series granted for local church use. Copyright © Group Publishing, Inc., P.O. Box 481, Loveland, CO 80539.

[handwritten notes in right margin: Holy Spirit — sadness that is used by God brings a b of heart that leads to salvation, sadness by humans brings death, motivates to prove innocence — If we confess our sins God keeps his promise, he forgives us of all our wrongdoing.]

GUILT TRIP ▼

Station 1: Alphabet Guilt
(10 to 15 minutes)
Have everyone line up against the Station 1 wall, then say: **Look at the letter on your hand. Think of something you've felt guilty about that starts with that letter.**

After a few moments, say: **When I call out the letter written on your hand, step forward.**

Call out one of the letters you wrote on kids' hands. After kids step forward, say: **Turn toward the group, and hold your lettered hand in front of your face, palm out. As you do this, think about the situation your letter represents.**

Time students for ten seconds, then allow them to return to their places. Repeat this process until everyone has displayed his or her letter. Then form pairs so kids can discuss these questions:

● **How did it feel to expose your letter to the group?**

● **How is exposing your letter like revealing your guilty feelings to others?**

● **Did you worry about others' responses even though no one knew what you were feeling guilty about? Why or why not?**

● **Why is it hard to discuss things you feel guilty about?**

When pairs finish, invite volunteers to tell the group what they

DEPTHFINDER — JOB'S TRUE AND FALSE GUILT

Job's story provides an excellent example of true guilt vs. false guilt. Job suffered many tragedies beyond his control, yet Job's three friends attacked him because they believed his problems were the result of a secret sinful lifestyle (Job 4–5; 8; and 11).

Job had two choices: accept what they said and repent or refute their accusations. Despite his weakened state, Job adamantly refuted his friends arguments and rejected the false guilt they tried to heap on him (Job 6–7; 9; and 12–14).

Even though Job wasn't guilty of the sin his friends accused him of, he was guilty of doubting God's ultimate authority. When God convicted Job of his sin, Job confessed and repented (Job 42:1-6). Job knew when he was truly guilty, and his repentance restored his relationship with God.

discussed. Then say: **As we move to our next station, think about other things in your life you've felt guilty about.**

Station 2: Guilt-O-Meters (15 to 20 minutes)

Once kids are at the next station, say: **We might feel guilty for a lot of reasons. Sometimes we feel true guilt—we've done something wrong or failed to do what was right. Other times we feel false guilt—we or others have unrealistic expectations that we haven't met. To learn the difference, we're going to study Job, a Bible character who encountered both.**

Job was caught in unfortunate circumstances. Job lost all he had, including his children and his health. To make things worse, people in Job's culture believed that if something bad happened to you, you must've sinned to cause it. So when this tragedy fell upon Job, three of his well-meaning friends decided to confront him for his "sinfulness."

Have kids form trios, and hand each trio a copy of the "Job's True and False Guilt" Depthfinder above. Say: **In your trios, read the handout I gave you. Then read Job 11:1-20 and 12:2-5. In the first passage, one of Job's friends confronts him, and in the second passage, Job responds to his friend's accusations.**

Then have trios discuss these questions:
- **What did Job's friend accuse him of?**
- **How did Job respond to his friend's accusations?**
- **Do you think Job felt guilty? Why or why not?**
- **Do you ever feel guilty for things that aren't your fault? Why or why not?**
- **What do you do when you feel guilty?**

While trios are talking, set out marbles, sandwich bags, string, tape, and poster board. Say: **Job's friends tried to heap false guilt on him—accusing him of being sinful when he wasn't. You may be able to relate to Job, feeling false guilt for things which aren't** your fault. For example, you might feel guilty because your parents have divorced, or a sibling has died, or you chose not to play basketball when your parents hoped you would.

In your trios, create a "machine" that represents false guilt. Choose one person in your trio to be the Base of the machine, then use the supplies I've provided to construct a machine that piles "false guilt" on your Base. For example, you could roll the poster board into a tube shape and funnel marbles into a bag attached to your Base. Be prepared to tell the rest of the group how your machine represents false guilt.

When trios are ready, invite them to demonstrate their machines and explain how they represent false guilt. Encourage groups to tell what they like about each other's creations. Then ask:

● **Bases, how did it feel to have false guilt heaped on you?**
● **The rest of you, how did it feel to weigh your Base down with false guilt?**
● **How is that feeling like what happens in real life?**

Then say: **Job's friends illustrate how even people with good intentions can make you feel false guilt.**

In their trios, have kids respond to these questions:
● **Do you ever feel false guilt? If so, for what?**
● **On a scale of one to ten, how much false guilt do you carry around every day?**

After trios respond, say: **Each of you take a sandwich bag and fill it with marbles based on your response to the last question. For example, if your answer was "eight," place eight marbles in your bag. Then use string to tie the bag and hang it around your neck like a necklace.**

When kids have finished their marble-bag necklaces, say: **False guilt makes us forget how special we are. For each marble in your bag, let your trio members tell you something good about who you are.**

When trios finish, have them gather near Station 3. Say: **Like the weight of the necklaces you now wear, false guilt can weigh you down. But** <u>**God can free you from feelings of guilt.**</u> **In the next experience, we're going to explore the differences between false and true guilt so we can let go of false guilt and seek God's forgiveness when we need it.**

Station 3: Heart Monitor (10 to 15 minutes)

Say: **Guilt makes us respond in funny ways. When we feel guilty, our behavior changes. We treat people differently—we avoid them or try to make up for what we've done.**

Give each student an index card and a pencil. Say: **On your card, write one memory that still makes you feel guilty. For example, you might feel guilty because you broke a plate when you were five. Or because you said something mean to a friend. Write it down, but do *not* write your name on the card.**

When kids have finished, collect the cards. Say: **When we feel guilty, we can often feel our hearts pounding faster, especially if** we think someone's going to find out what we did. We're now going to create a "heart monitor" to determine how guilty we feel about different situations.

Designate one corner of the room as "racing-heart corner" and the opposite corner as "resting-heart corner." Say: **I'm going to read some of your cards. As I read each situation, move to the appropriate place in the room to indicate how guilty you'd feel about this situation. For example, if you'd feel really guilty about a situation, go to the racing-heart corner. If you wouldn't feel guilty at all, go to the resting-heart corner. If you'd feel somewhat guilty, stand somewhere between the two corners.**

Randomly choose three or four cards, then read them aloud one at a time, allowing kids to respond to each card by moving to a different place in the room. After you read each card, have kids each turn to a partner and explain why they chose to stand where they are.

After the activity, have kids return to their trios and give each group a copy of the "True or False?" Depthfinder (p. 29). Have trios read the Depthfinder and study the passages listed. Then have trios answer these questions:

● **Based on what you just read, do you feel true guilt or false guilt for the thing you wrote on your card earlier? Explain.**

● **If we were to do this activity again, would you change where you stood for any of the situations? Why or why not?**

● **What causes you to feel false guilt? true guilt?**

● **What's the difference in how you respond to false guilt and true guilt?**

Say: **We've already read about Job's response to false guilt. But Job felt true guilt also. He doubted that God was in control of his life because so many bad things had happened to him. God confronted Job about Job's lack of faith. God also confronted Job's friends for what they said to Job about God. In your trios, read Job 42:1-11 to see how Job and his friends responded to their true guilt.**

Have trios discuss these questions:

● **How did Job and his friends respond to true guilt?**

● **How was Job's response to true guilt different from his response to false guilt?**

● **How did Job and his friends' responses to true guilt affect their relationships with God?**

● **How do you respond when you feel true guilt?**

● **How does your response affect your relationship with God?**

Randomly pass back the index cards to your students, and ask each student to tape a card to his or her clothes. Say: **Sometimes we feel guilty for things that aren't sins—we feel false guilt. But other times, we truly are guilty for doing something wrong or not** doing something right. <u>God can free you from feelings of</u> 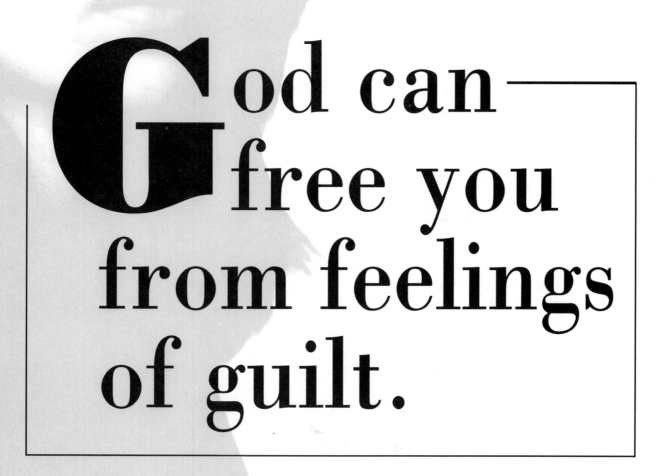 <u>guilt.</u> **In our last activity, we'll see how.**

UNPACKING AND DEBRIEFING ▼

Wipe It Out (5 to 10 minutes)
Have kids form a circle. Say: **James 5:16 tells us that when we have real guilt, we should confess our sins to each other. Let's do that for the guilt objects we now carry.**

Form pairs, and have each student tell a partner one thing in life that provokes guilty feelings.

Then distribute clean rags, and set out the bowl of soapy water. Invite pairs to "wipe out" each other's guilt by washing the letters off their partners' hands. Have kids remove their partners' necklaces and the index cards from their partners' clothes.

When pairs finish, have them pray together asking God to help them release true and false guilt in their lives.

God can free you from feelings of guilt.

Face the Light

Helping Kids Turn to God When They Make Mistakes

by Erin McKay

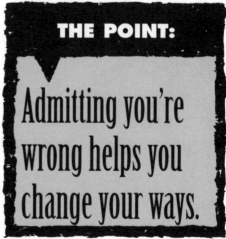

THE POINT:

Admitting you're wrong helps you change your ways.

■ Kids live in a world that glorifies human endeavor and achievement. By the time they finish grade school, most kids have learned to tout their strengths and hide their weaknesses in order to be accepted and admired. By watching others cover up their mistakes, it's easy for kids to come to the conclusion that admirable people either don't make mistakes or don't get caught making them. ■ But refusal to admit our mistakes distances us from God. It trivializes sin and it leads to doubts about our relationship and standing before God. Romans 3:23-24 explains that "all have sinned and fall short of the glory of God, and are justified freely by his grace through the redemption that came by Christ Jesus." Repentance brings restoration. Only by turning from our sin and turning towards the salvation of Jesus, can we be changed.

The Study
AT A GLANCE

SECTION	MINUTES	WHAT STUDENTS WILL DO	SUPPLIES
Learning Game	5 to 10	CUP-TO-CUP RELAY—Participate in a race to see that making mistakes in life is inevitable.	Bucket, warm water, measuring spoons, laundry detergent, white vinegar, old sheet, fruit juice, paper cups, table
Learning Activity	5 to 10	HIDE AND SEE—Search for "hidden" images and compare the activity to detecting sin in our lives.	Magic Eye 3-D pictures
Bible Exploration	25 to 30	TREASURE HUNT—Use clues to search for a hidden treasure and analyze Bible verses that describe man's need for—and God's response to—true repentance.	Bibles, "Clues" handouts (pp. 43-44), "Mistake Tokens" handouts (p. 45), scissors, tape, bag, cupcakes or cookies, pencils, paper
Personal Application	5 to 10	LIST 'EM AND LEAVE 'EM—Recall and ask forgiveness for past mistakes and tear up reminders of their sins.	Bible, pencils, Mistake Tokens from "Treasure Hunt" activity, sheet from "Cup-to-Cup Relay" activity

notes:

Admitting you're wrong helps you change your ways.

THE BIBLE CONNECTION

PSALM 103:8-12; ISAIAH 1:18; MARK 2:17	These passages assure us of God's forgiveness.
PROVERBS 28:13; LUKE 15:8-10; 2 CORINTHIANS 7:10-11; HEBREWS 9:9-10; 1 JOHN 1:8-10	These passages show how sin should be dealt with.
HEBREWS 4:13	This verse explains that God is omniscient.

In this study, kids will participate in a race while trying not to stain a cloth. They'll search for "hidden" images and then go on a treasure hunt while trying to avoid making mistakes. Kids will then repent of their sins.

BEFORE THE STUDY

For the "Cup-to-Cup Relay" activity, mix a stain-removal solution of one quart warm water, one teaspoon laundry detergent, and one tablespoon white vinegar in a bucket. Also drape a white bedsheet over a table.

For the "Hide and See" activity, collect Magic Eye pictures from newspapers' Sunday comics sections.

For the "Treasure Hunt" activity, think of clues that will lead your kids to specific areas of your building or the surrounding area. The first clue should lead kids to the second clue. The second clue should lead kids to the third clue and so forth. Write the clues in the spaces provided on the "Clues" handout (pp. 43-44), and make one copy for every two kids in your class. Cut the clues into separate strips, and tape one copy each of Clue #2 through Clue #5 in the area described by the previous clue. For example, if Clue #1 leads kids to the drinking fountain, make certain Clue #2 is hidden near the fountain. Keep the remainder of the clue copies for later use. Bake or buy enough cupcakes or cookies for everyone in your class. Place two of these treats in a small bag, tape one copy of Clue #6 to the bag, and hide the treats. For every two kids in your class, make one copy of the "Mistake Tokens" handout (p. 45), and cut out the tokens. Store the rest of the treats where kids won't discover them.

THE STUDY

LEARNING GAME ▼

Cup-to-Cup Relay (5 to 10 minutes)

After kids arrive, explain that this lesson is about turning to God when we sin. Have the class form two teams, and ask them to stand on opposite sides of a table and face each other. Give each player a paper cup. Pour juice into the cups of the two opposing players at one end of the table. Join one of the teams, and explain that when you say "go," the first person on each team will pour the juice from his or her cup into the next person's cup. That person will pour the juice into the next person's cup, and so on, until the juice has been poured from cup to cup all the way down the line and back again.

Explain that the goal is for one team to finish the relay first with the most juice left in its cup. Remind kids to do their pouring over the sheet and to pour as fast as they can. If the kids don't spill a drop of juice onto the sheet, make certain you do.

When the game is over, say: **We've all made messes in the past. None of us is perfect, and we all sin. Imagine for a moment that this sheet represents your life and the stains are the sins you've committed.** Ask:

- **In what way are the sins you've committed like these stains?**
- **How are they different?**
- **If you were looking at your life through God's eyes, would it have more stains or fewer stains than this sheet?**
- **Is a mistake the same thing as a sin? Explain.**

LEADER TIP for Cup-to-Cup Relay

Before this activity, test the bedsheet material and the juice brand you plan to use to make certain the stain-removal solution will work. The solution does work with cotton sheets and bottled Libby's Juicy Juice—100% Fruit Juice (apple and grape juice mix), and Shurfine frozen Cranberry-Raspberry Juice Cocktail.

"If we claim to be without sin, we deceive ourselves and the truth is not in us. If we confess our sins, he is faithful and just and will forgive us our sins and purify us from all unrighteousness."

—1 John 1:8-9

DEPTH FINDER   SIN MATTERS

Because we're all guilty of sin and the world is full of sin, it's easy to be complacent about it. Kids need to know that sin is much more offensive to God than it is to us. To put it bluntly, God *hates* sin. Romans 6:23 says, "For the wages of sin is death." This is why Jesus paid for our sins with his life. To young Christians especially, this judgment might sound harsh. It's important for them to understand that God *is* purity and *is* righteousness; he cannot tolerate evil. As a holy God, he cannot overlook sin and pretend it doesn't exist.

In his book *Know What You Believe*, Paul E. Little describes the connection between God's holiness and God's justice: "It is important to realize...that God exercises all His attributes in harmony with each other. His holiness demands atonement for sin. His love provides it." Little goes on to say: "Sin makes a real difference to God, and even in forgiving, He cannot ignore sin or regard it as other or less than it is."

Say: **When we make mistakes that offend God, we sin against him. Some of the sins we commit are very visible, like these stains. Other sins are not easily seen—either we're good at hiding them or we don't know that we've offended God! Sometimes sin can be hard to detect. But it's important for us to recognize our sin because admitting you're wrong helps you change your ways.**

Immerse the sheet in the bucket of stain-removal solution you made before the study, and let it soak while you proceed with the rest of the lesson.

LEARNING ACTIVITY ▼

Hide and See
(5 to 10 minutes)

Hold up the Magic Eye pictures you collected before the study and ask:

● **How many of you have tried to find the hidden images in computer-generated graphics like these?**

Pass the pictures around, explain the techniques for seeing the images, and give kids a few minutes to find them.

After everyone has had a chance to search for a 3-D image, ask kids whether they thought this activity was easy or difficult. Say: **Sometimes our sins are not as visible as stains on a sheet. For human beings, seeing the sin in our own lives can be like trying to find the 3-D images in these pictures. Let's hear what the Bible has to say about *God's* ability to see sin.**

Ask a volunteer to read aloud Hebrews 4:13. Ask:

● **Why do you think it's important to ask for forgiveness if God sees all our sins anyway?**

● **What kinds of sins are difficult for us to see? easy for us to see?**

● **How does it feel to apologize to people? to God?**

LEADER TIP for Hide and See

Three-dimensional Magic Eye illusions, created by N.E. Thing Enterprises, are distributed by Universal Press Syndicate and appear in many newspapers' Sunday comics. Many bookstores and libraries also carry Magic Eye books, published by Andrews and McMeel, 4900 Main St., Kansas City, MO 64112.

There are two recommended methods for seeing Magic Eye 3-D images:

● Hold the picture close to your face, relax your eyes, and focus on a point "beyond" the picture. Slowly move it away from your face and keep staring "through" it until the 3-D image becomes apparent.

● If the Magic Eye picture is printed on glossy paper, hold it so that you can see an object being reflected. Fix your gaze on the object until you see depth in the Magic Eye picture.

DEPTH FINDER — DANGEROUS PRIDE

The Bible is full of stories about man's inability to see his own sin. Ironically, the very people who strive to know God and to do his will are especially susceptible to this kind of blindness. In Luke 18:9-14, Jesus tells the story of a Pharisee and a corrupt tax collector who went to the Temple to pray. The Pharisee thanked God for making him more righteous than the tax collector, while the tax collector begged God for forgiveness. According to Jesus, the tax collector—not the Pharisee—returned home forgiven.

Kids need to be reminded that pride can come between themselves and God's mercy. God, who knows the secrets of every heart and understands our motives, can see sin we cannot see ourselves. The more we ask God to show us our wrongdoing, the better able we are to recognize and change our offensive behavior and faulty thinking. In a world that exalts self-confidence and self-esteem, kids need to know that a good relationship with God requires honesty and a healthy dose of humility.

● **What does our society say we should do about our sins? Explain.**
● **How does it feel to have someone apologize to you when they aren't really sorry for what they've done?**
● **Do we have to be sorry for our sins before God will help us?**
Say: **No matter how good we try to be, we're all guilty of sin. God wants us to be genuinely sorry for the mistakes we've made. When we repent, God forgives us. In fact, God says he will forget our sins as if they never happened! His forgiveness brings true healing and genuine change. It's amazing and wonderful how admitting you're wrong helps you change your ways.**

BIBLE EXPLORATION ▼

LEADER TIP for Treasure Hunt

Create clues that will send kids in different directions throughout the area. For example, if you have more than one exit sign in your building, create a clue that will lead kids to the signs.

Treasure Hunt (25 to 30 minutes)

Have kids form pairs. Give each pair a Bible and a pencil. Say: **You and your partner are going to go on a treasure hunt by following clues. I'll give you the first clue that will lead to the second clue. If your pair finds the second clue, remove it, look up the Bible verse on it, write down the answer to the question, and search for the third clue. You must answer the question before moving on to the next clue.**

If your pair finds a clue, don't return it for others to use. The teams who don't find a clue must come to me to receive the clue and a Mistake Token. Even if you get the clue from me, you must look up the Bible verse and write down the answer to the question before you move on. Continue searching for clues until the treasure is found.

Tell kids that partners must stay together and that talking between pairs is not allowed. Once the treasure has been found, have kids come back together. If the treasure has not been found after fifteen minutes, have kids come back together, and give a copy of Clue #5 to

DEPTH FINDER — MERCIFUL GOD

LEADER TIP
for Treasure Hunt

If you have an opportunity to use a large area for this activity, provide boundaries so your kids don't wander too far away from your meeting area.

Your kids may be familiar with the story of Jonah and the whale. At first, Jonah refused to warn the people of Nineveh, as God had directed him. He ran away, hiding in the bottom of a boat bound for Tarshish. But God caused the sea to grow rough. The men on the boat threw Jonah overboard, and he was swallowed up by a great fish as God had arranged.

The story of Jonah is a story about forgiveness. While in the belly of the fish, Jonah cried out to God and was spit out onto dry land. Again God directed Jonah to go to Nineveh. This time Jonah obeyed. Consequently the people of Nineveh repented of their sins, and God forgave them.

Just as God was merciful toward Jonah and the inhabitants of Nineveh, he is merciful toward us. All that he requires of us is a contrite heart. In Jonah's case, God even provided the storm and the fish—practically guaranteeing Jonah's repentance!

all the pairs. Ask the winning pair to show the treasure to the rest of the class and consume the treasure. Then surprise everyone by providing treats for the rest of the class.

While kids enjoy their snacks, have each pair share one answer to the questions under the clues. Then ask:

- **Was it difficult to know when to come to me for help?**
- **How did you feel when I gave you a Mistake Token?**
- **What happened if you waited a long time to admit you were on the wrong track?**
- **How did you feel when you heard or saw other teams find the clues before you did?**
- **Why do you think it's difficult for us to admit when we're wrong?**
- **Why do you think repentance is so important to God?**

Say: **Admitting you're wrong helps you change your ways.**  **Repentance is the first step to true change and growth. When we're too proud to come to God for his help, we force ourselves to continue in damaging behavior. When we let go of our pride and admit our errors, we give God the opportunity to begin the process of change in our hearts and to point us in the right direction.**

LEADER TIP
for Treasure Hunt

If the lesson must be conducted within a confined area, kids can play a written version of the game. To do this, have kids guess the imaginary location of each clue until they "find" the treasure. Teams can guess as many times as they want (submitting their answers on pieces of paper) but should receive a Mistake Token for every incorrect guess. When a team guesses correctly, the leader should give that team the next clue.

PERSONAL APPLICATION ▼

List 'Em and Leave 'Em
(5 to 10 minutes)
Have kids redistribute their Mistake Tokens so every person has one. Then have everyone spread out and write on the back of the tokens things they're sorry they've done or neglected to do. After a few minutes, have a volunteer read aloud Psalm 103:8-12.

Ask:
- **How should our sins be punished?**
- **Do you see God as forgiving or judging? Why?**

LEADER TIP

for List 'Em and
Leave 'Em

As you lift the bed-
sheet out of the stain-
removal solution, be
careful not to allow
the water to stain your
carpet.

● **Is it ever difficult for you to believe that your sins have been removed as far as the east is from west? Explain.**

Lift the bedsheet that's been soaking in the stain-removal solution, and show it to the class. Say: **Remember how soiled this was after we played the first game? Every time someone goofed and spilled some juice, it left a stain. In the same way, our sins cause spiritual stains. When we sin, sometimes we can make amends and sometimes we can't. But whenever we admit that we have done something wrong, and we are truly sorry, God promises to forgive us.** Ask a volunteer to read aloud Isaiah 1:18.

Have kids return to their pairs from the "Treasure Hunt" activity and then spread out around the room. Encourage kids to ask God for forgiveness for the sins written on their tokens. Explain that if they feel comfortable doing so, they can confess their sins to their partners and pray together, or they can choose to confess and pray silently. When kids finish praying, have them stand up, tear their tokens into pieces, and throw them in the air. Have partners remind each other that their sins have been forgiven.

Pray: **Heavenly Father, thank you for being a merciful God who does not hold grudges. Thank you for not expecting us to be perfect and for being so patient with us. We're sorry for these sins that we have committed. Thank you for removing them from us as far as the east is from the west. Help us to** admit when we're wrong so that we can change our ways. **In Jesus' name, amen.**

Thank kids for coming to class, and tell them to leave their sins behind.

Clues

Clue #1

Read Hebrews 9:9-10.

Why do sacrifices fail to cleanse our hearts?

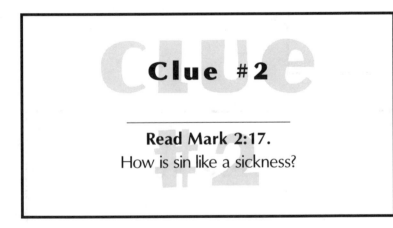

Clue #2

Read Mark 2:17.

How is sin like a sickness?

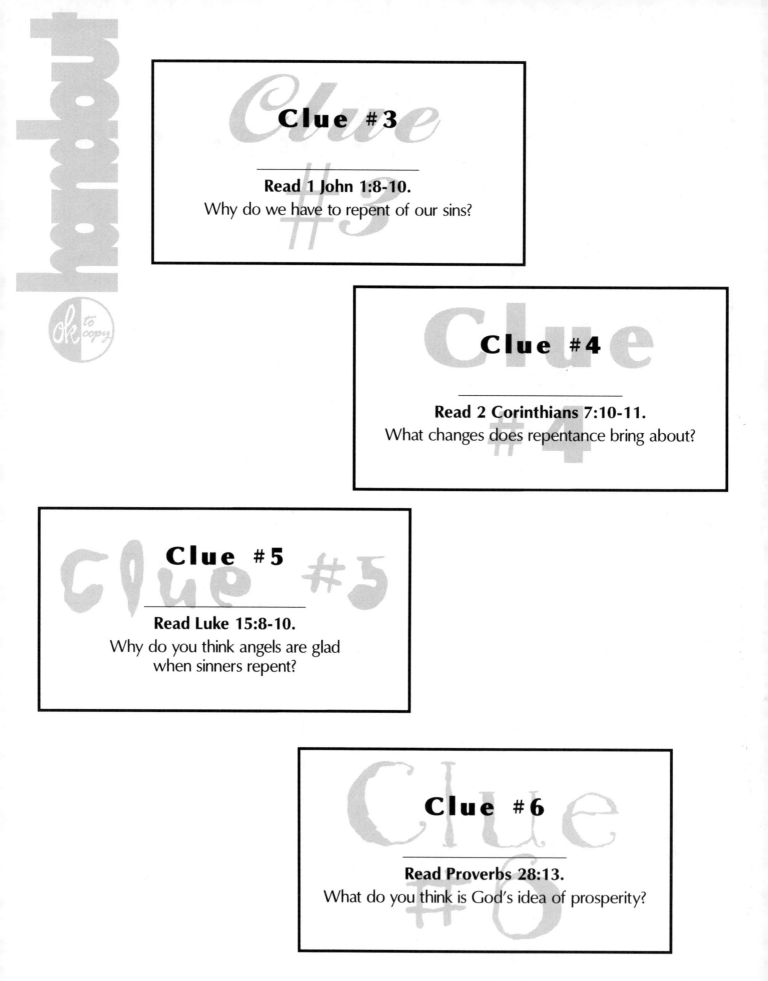

Clue #3

Read 1 John 1:8-10.
Why do we have to repent of our sins?

Clue #4

Read 2 Corinthians 7:10-11.
What changes does repentance bring about?

Clue #5

Read Luke 15:8-10.
Why do you think angels are glad
when sinners repent?

Clue #6

Read Proverbs 28:13.
What do you think is God's idea of prosperity?

Mistake Tokens

Dennis 9-9-01

A Veiled Threat

Helping Kids Guard Their Hearts and Minds

by **Pamela J. Shoup**

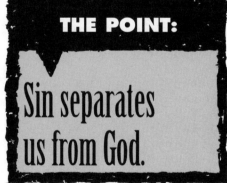

THE POINT:

Sin separates us from God.

■ Today's teenagers still believe in the American dream. But is their version of the dream mere fantasy? In *Understanding Today's Youth Culture*, Walt Mueller writes that the media bombards teenagers with the message that money, good looks, travel to exotic places, expensive cars and clothing can and should be theirs. But nowhere does the media tell them that what they really need is a relationship with God through Christ. ■ Not all dreams and fantasies are evil or negative. Fantasy can help kids reach for the future and set goals. But if it goes unchecked, fantasy can cloud their vision by cloaking reality and offering an unrealistic and inflated sense of self—with no room for God in their lives. ■ In this study teenagers will explore and analyze their fantasies and dreams as they relate to Scripture to feed and condition their minds for spiritual excellence.

The Study
AT A GLANCE

SECTION	MINUTES	WHAT STUDENTS WILL DO	SUPPLIES
Opener	10 to 15	FANTASY ISLAND—Choose a fantasy identity and role-play that character.	Index cards, markers, masking tape
Bible Exploration	5 to 10	FANTASY TRAP—Discuss true stories where people were trapped by their fantasies	Bibles
	20 to 25	GUARDING YOUR HEART AND MIND—Gain tools to evaluate fantasies and media messages.	Bibles, index cards from "Fantasy Island" activity, paper, pencils, "A Christian's Tool Kit" handouts (pp. 55-56), newsprint, tape, marker
Closing	5 to 10	HOPE-DREAMS—Share their positive dreams for the future.	Bibles, paper, markers

notes:

Sin separates us from God.

THE BIBLE CONNECTION

2 CORINTHIANS 10:3-5	Paul explains the methods for fighting spiritual and mental battles.
PHILIPPIANS 4:8	Paul explains what the Christian thought life should be like.
JAMES 1:14-15	James explains that sin begins with evil thoughts and desires.

In this study kids will compare their fantasies and dreams to Scriptural teachings of true, right, and pure thinking. Kids will develop practical filters for deciding what to occupy their minds with and how to dream about the future.

By exploring the thought life, each student will learn that fantasies and dreams can be positive and faith-building or obsessive and destructive.

Explore the verses in The Bible Connection, then examine the information in the Depthfinder boxes throughout the study to gain a deeper understanding of how these Scriptures connect with your young people.

THE STUDY

LEADER TIP *for The Study*

Because this topic can be so powerful and relevant to kids' lives, your group members may be tempted to get caught up in issues and lose sight of the deeper biblical principle found in The Point. Help your kids grasp The Point by guiding kids to focus on the biblical investigation and discussing how God's truth connects with reality in their lives.

OPENER ▼

Fantasy Island (10 to 15 minutes)
When everyone has arrived, say: **Welcome to Fantasy Island! Today we're going to explore some of your fantasies and dreams. In this first activity, you can be whoever you want to be. So start thinking about your fantasy identity.** Set out index cards and markers, and tell each student to write on an index card the name of a person, real or imagined, who he or she might like to be. Explain that each student can choose to be a famous athlete, movie star, superhero, mythical character, political figure—anything he

LEADER TIP for The Study

Whenever groups discuss a list of questions, write the questions on newsprint, and tape the newsprint to a wall so groups can discuss the questions at their own pace.

or she chooses. Ask kids to keep their characters' names secret. Then pass around a roll of masking tape, and have kids tape the index cards to the front of their shirts.

Say: **First, cover your character's name with your hand. Now walk around the room and act out your character. As you engage in conversation, give other students clues about who you are. Once someone guesses your identity, uncover your character's name. After you find out your classmates' characters, treat them as those characters.** Give kids a few minutes to interact as their fantasy characters. Gather everyone together and ask:

● **What was it like to pretend to be someone else?**
● **How did you choose who you wanted to be?**
● **If you were rich, powerful, famous, had super powers, or could do fantastic things, do you think you could still be a good person? Why or why not?**
● **How are your fantasies affected by the movies you watch, video games you play, books you read, or music you listen to?**

Ask kids to keep their index cards for use in a later activity.

Say: **It's fun to dream about what we could be and about what we will become. But some fantasies can be dangerous because they lead to sin. Since <u>sin separates us from God,</u> we need to avoid any type of thought or fantasy that will cause confusion in our relationship with him.**

BIBLE EXPLORATION ▼

Fantasy Trap (5 to 10 minutes) Say: **God has given us the gifts of imagination and dreaming to provide us with hope for our future. But like most gifts, imagination and dreaming can be twisted into horrible experiences. Consider these true stories.**

Read: **As a boy, Ted Bundy was a Boy Scout and an A student. He grew into a handsome, intelligent young man, went to law school, and seemed headed for a career in politics. But Ted Bundy was hooked on pornography and became one of our country's most notorious and vicious serial killers. Just before he was executed in the electric chair in 1989, Bundy said his violent fantasies were fueled by pornography.** (Source: Time magazine, Feb. 6, 1989.)

Pause for a few seconds, then read: **Dallas Egbert was described as a genius. At sixteen years old, he attended Michigan State University as a sophomore. Michigan State had an intricate system of tunnels for steam pipes and hidden rooms under the campus. People who played the role-play game Dungeons and Dragons would sometimes use the tunnels to act out their games. Dallas was one of these students, and it was after one of the games in the tunnels that he was found missing.**

Dallas' parents hired William Dear to find Dallas. After exten-

DEPTHFINDER

UNDERSTANDING YOUR TEENAGERS

Ask your teenagers what their fantasies are, and the most common answer should involve some sort of travel, often to a tropical island, and usually with someone of the opposite sex according to *The Private Life of the American Teenager* by Jane Norman and Myron Harris.

"It is obvious that their fantasies are not too dissimilar from ours. They relish escape from the daily confrontations and pressures we all experience," Norman and Harris say.

Kids from divorced families often fantasize about spending time with the absent parent in a real or idyllic setting. Many of teenagers' daydreams also involve achievements in sports such as making the winning basket in a big game, or having glamorous careers.

"Fantasies and dreams are not meaningless," the authors say. "They kindle the creativity that keeps us searching for more satisfying ways of living. Adolescents share our reluctance to accept final limitations on life. They refuse to settle for the dictates of a society that says, 'This is the way it is, accept it.' If we scorn their aspirations for a better world by insisting that their dreams are idealistic or unrealistic, we may merely be revealing our own failures and sense of discouragement. But if our teenagers work toward change, they just might attain it. These teenagers still believe in the American dream."

But fantasies can become abnormal or even harmful. If a daydream becomes an obsession, it's time to get help. Chronic daydreaming can also prevent people from going out and taking risks since they have an excuse to stay in dreamland.

"Unfortunately, life can never be as good as a fantasy. And if you live too much in a dream world, you're always disappointed in life," according to the 'Teen magazine article "What Do Your Daydreams Reveal?" by Andrea Heiman (September 1996).

sive searching, Dear found the runaway young man but with a very different personality. After being found, Dallas wrote a letter containing the statement, "I'll give Satan my mind and power." Dallas sank into a state of deep depression for the next year which led to his suicide. (Adapted from Joan Hake Robie's *The Truth About Dungeons and Dragons.)*

Have kids form groups of three or four and sit with their groups to discuss the following questions:

● **Do you think that pornography had anything to do with Ted Bundy's horrendous crimes against women? Why or why not?**

● **Do you think the fantasy game Dungeons and Dragons had anything to do with Dallas Egbert's suicide? Why or why not?**

● **In what ways can fantasy be a bad thing?**

● **In what ways can fantasy be a good thing?**

● **Read James 1:14-15. How do these verses apply to the two stories? to our everyday thoughts and fantasies?**

● **How can you avoid the traps of negative and evil fantasy?**

● **Read 2 Corinthians 10:3-5. In the stories you heard, what might have come from the forces of evil in the world?**

● **What are some of God's weapons we can use to fight evil** thoughts and fantasies?

● If you are trapped in destructive fantasy behavior, how can you get out?

Say: **Some fantasy, when it includes evil thoughts or takes over your life, can cloud your vision. It gives you an unrealistic view of yourself and the world and can cause you to sin. Sin separates us from God. But God always offers us forgiveness when we confess our sins. Unrealistic fantasies and dreams take away from the glory of God. Goals, aspirations, and dreams can give you hope for the future and bring you closer to God. Let's look at some tools you can use to guard your hearts and your minds.**

Guarding Your Heart and Mind (20 to 25 minutes)

Have kids stay with their groups and get their index cards from the opening activity. Distribute paper and pencils to all the students.

Assign one of the following forms of entertainment to each group: a video game, the Internet, a song, a daydream, a show on television, a movie, a book, or a music video.

Say: **With your group, think of a specific example of the form of entertainment you've been assigned. For example, if your group has been assigned a book, you might use *The Grapes of Wrath* as your example.**

Distribute a copy of the "Christian's Tool Kit" handout (pp. 55-56) to each person.

Say: **With your groups, follow the directions on the handout to evaluate your fantasy identity on your index card and your group's chosen example. Write down your answers as you work. No one else will see your papers, so please be honest with yourself.**

Give groups about ten minutes to complete the handouts. Gather everyone back together and ask:

● **What are some ways that we can keep our thoughts true, right, pure, and lovely?**

● **Does anyone wish you'd chosen another type of character for your fantasy identity? Explain.**

● **How did your example of the form of entertainment you were assigned measure up to the evaluation guidelines?**

● **How will this evaluation affect what you watch or read or listen to in the future?**

Tape a sheet of newsprint to a wall. Ask kids to shout out other things they think could lead to negative fantasies and things they think they probably shouldn't spend time dreaming and thinking about. As kids offer suggestions, write them on the sheet of newsprint. Ask:

● **How can these things lead to negative fantasies?**
● **How can they lead to a positive thought-life?**
● **How can we know when to avoid these things?**
● **What should we do when we find ourselves struggling with negative fantasies and thoughts?**

Say: **Be a wise media consumer by taking time to know God's**

DEPTHFINDER — THE BATTLE WITH SATAN

Everyone fantasizes occasionally about weird things. Healthy people give themselves a reality-check and shake off anything that seems destructive or even evil. But sometimes even strong Christians have perverse thoughts, or fleeting doubts cross their minds about God. Those kinds of thoughts result from Satan's battle for more control in this world.

According to Neil Anderson and Rich Miller in their book *Know Light, No Fear*, kids have to understand that there is a battle between good and evil going on for the control of their minds. Dreams, voices, or visions we encounter can come from Satan as easily as they can come from God.

In a survey of 1,700 professing Christian junior and senior high students, Anderson and Steve Russo (authors of *The Seduction of Our Children*) found that

- 48 percent said they had experienced some presence in their room that scared them,
- 50 percent said they have had bad thoughts about God,
- about one-third said that it is hard for them to concentrate while praying and reading the Bible,
- nearly one of five said they frequently had thoughts of suicide, and
- over 20 percent have had impulsive thoughts to kill somebody.

Anderson and Russo explain that when these things happen to your teenagers, they are under spiritual attack. Every temptation of Satan is an attempt to get us to think only of *our* needs and to grow apart from God. Tell your teenagers, "You can defeat the devil in the battle for your mind, because Christ has already won the war."

Anderson and Miller believe the devil's trickiest tactic is neither temptation nor accusation, but rather deception.

"The devil is a liar (John 8:44), and he is constantly seeking to lead our minds astray from the truth. That's why you need to know the truth, because 'the truth will set you free' (John 8:32). You need to walk with Jesus, because he is 'the way and the truth and the life' (John 14:6). You need to be filled with the Holy Spirit who is the 'Spirit of truth,' who will 'guide you into all truth' (John 16:13)."

Your teenagers need tools so they aren't fooled by the thin veil of deception. Using this study, you can equip your teenagers with the knowledge and tools to fight the forces of evil in this world and teach them to make good decisions about what they take into their minds. And sometimes you just have to reassure your teenagers that you think about weird things, too.

Word and to apply it through critical viewing and thinking. <u>Sin separates us from God.</u> And if we guard our hearts and minds from temptation and sin, we can focus our thoughts on God and grow in our spiritual lives.

Close this activity with a prayer of your own or with this one:

Dear God, give us wisdom to know what we should be thinking about and to know when what we're thinking or fantasizing about is wrong. We ask your Holy Spirit to guide us in thinking about things that are true, noble, right, pure, lovely, admirable, excellent, and praiseworthy so we may grow closer to you and avoid sin and temptation. Amen.

X **Hope-Dreams** (5 to 10 minutes)

Say: **Now we're going to do some time travel. Let's go about twenty years in the future. Where are you? What are you doing? Let's draw our "hope-dreams"—what you truly hope to be doing twenty years from now.**

Distribute markers and paper. Have kids create a picture that represents who they'll be and what they'll be doing in twenty years. After a few minutes, have kids find a partner to share their pictures with. Tell partners to share their dreams and the steps they plan to take to achieve those dreams.

Have kids stay with their partners, but ask the following questions to the whole group:

● **Does your dream for the future meet the guidelines in Philippians 4:8? What is good about your dream?**

● **How are these dreams different from the fantasies in the first activity? How are they similar?**

● **How do you think your dreams are realistic or unrealistic?**

Take a few minutes for kids each to share with the entire group why they think their partners will achieve their dreams.

Say: **Negative dreams and fantasies lead to sin, and <u>sin separates us from God.</u> Positive and pure thoughts and dreams can give you a sense of hope for the future and what you might achieve. My hope for all of you is that you continue to grow closer to God and always find ways to glorify him in your future with pure and honorable thoughts and dreams.**

Encourage your teenagers to take home the "Christian's Tool Kit" handout to evaluate what they see, hear, read, and play as it relates to their fantasies and real-life actions.

"But each one is tempted when, by his own evil desire, he is dragged away and enticed. Then, after desire has conceived, it gives birth to sin; and sin, when it is full-grown, gives birth to death."

—James 1:14-15

A Christian's Tool Kit

Guarding Your Heart and Mind

i Read Philippians 4:8.

2. Take your fantasy identity card and a sheet of paper. Write on the paper how your fantasy character meets the guidelines of this Scripture. For example, write what is true about your fantasy person, what is noble, what is right, what is pure, and so on.

"Finally, brothers, whatever is TRUE, whatever is NOBLE, whatever is RIGHT, whatever is PURE, whatever is LOVELY, whatever is ADMIRABLE—if anything is excellent or praiseworthy—think about such things."

3. With your group discuss these questions:

- How closely did your fantasy characters match this Scripture? How did they conflict with this verse?

- How can you choose to think about and dwell on good things rather than evil things?

- How can thinking about good things help you grow in your spiritual life?

—Philippians 4:8

4. With your group, evaluate the specific example you chose from your assigned form of entertainment by following these steps:

a. Discover. Ask yourself about your example:

● What does it say about God?

● What does it say about humanity?

● Is God replaced by some other deity (self, money, etc.)?

● Is it hopeful or hopeless?

● What does it say about the nature of sexuality?

● What character traits are promoted as positive? negative?

● How is beauty and personal worth established and defined?

● What world and life view is behind what I am seeing and hearing?

b. Discern. Evaluate what you have discovered in Step A and whether it measures up to God's Word. Instead of evaluating it on your own personal taste or preference, use critical biblical thinking.

c. Decide. If what you are observing or hearing is in agreement with God's Word, enjoy! But if it contradicts what God has said, ask yourself these questions:

● Should I listen or watch or play or read?

● Will I listen or watch or play or read?

(Source for the above three-step evaluation is *Understanding Today's Youth Culture* by Walt Mueller © 1994. Used by permission of Tyndale House Publishers, Inc. All rights reserved.)

why ▼Active and Interactive Learning works with teenagers

Let's Start With the Big Picture

Think back to a major life lesson you've learned.

Got it? Now answer these questions:

● Did you learn your lesson from something you read?

● Did you learn it from something you heard?

● Did you learn it from something you experienced?

If you're like 99 percent of your peers, you answered "yes" only to the third question—you learned your life lesson from something you experienced.

This simple test illustrates the most convincing reason for using active and interactive learning with young people: People learn best through experience. Or to put it even more simply, people learn by doing.

Learning by doing is what active learning is all about. No more sitting quietly in chairs and listening to a speaker expound theories about God—that's passive learning. Active learning gets kids out of their chairs and into the experience of life. With active learning, kids get to *do* what they're studying. They *feel* the effects of the principles you teach. They *learn* by experiencing truth firsthand.

Active learning works because it recognizes three basic learning needs and uses them in concert to enable young people to make discoveries on their own and to find practical life applications for the truths they believe.

So what are these three basic learning needs?

1. Teenagers need action.

2. Teenagers need to think.

3. Teenagers need to talk.

Read on to find out exactly how these needs will be met by using the active and interactive learning techniques in Group's Core Belief Bible Study Series in your youth group.

1. Teenagers Need Action

Aircraft pilots know well the difference between passive and active learning. Their passive learning comes through listening to flight instructors and reading flight-instruction books. Their active learning comes through actually flying an airplane or flight simulator. Books and lectures may be helpful, but pilots really learn to fly by manipulating a plane's controls themselves.

We can help young people learn in a similar way. Though we may engage students passively in some reading and listening to teachers, their understanding and application of God's Word will really take off through simulated and real-life experiences.

Forms of active learning include simulation games; role-plays; service projects; experiments; research projects; group pantomimes; mock trials; construction projects; purposeful games; field trips; and, of course, the most powerful form of active learning—real-life experiences.

We can more fully explain active learning by exploring four of its characteristics:

● **Active learning is an adventure.** Passive learning is almost always predictable. Students sit passively while the teacher or speaker follows a planned outline or script.

In active learning, kids may learn lessons the teacher never envisioned. Because the leader trusts students to help create the learning experience, learners may venture into unforeseen discoveries. And often the teacher learns as much as the students.

● **Active learning is fun and captivating.** What are we communicating when we say, "OK, the fun's over—time to talk about God"? What's the hidden message? That joy is separate from God? And that learning is separate from joy?

What a shame.

Active learning is not joyless. One seventh-grader we interviewed clearly remembered her best Sunday school lesson: "Jesus was the light, and we went into a dark room and shut off the lights. We had a candle, and we learned that Jesus is the light and the dark can't shut off the light." That's active learning. Deena enjoyed the lesson. She had fun. And she learned.

Active learning intrigues people. Whether they find a foot-washing experience captivating or maybe a bit uncomfortable, they learn. And they learn on a level deeper than any work sheet or teacher's lecture could ever reach.

● **Active learning involves everyone.** Here the difference between passive and active learning becomes abundantly clear. It's like the difference between watching a football game on television and actually playing in the game.

The "trust walk" provides a good example of involving everyone in active learning. Half of the group members put on blindfolds; the other half serve as guides. The "blind" people trust the guides to lead them through the building or outdoors. The guides prevent the blind people from falling down stairs or tripping over rocks. Everyone needs to participate to learn the inherent lessons of trust, faith, doubt, fear, confidence, and servanthood. Passive spectators of this experience would learn little, but participants learn a great deal.

● **Active learning is focused through debriefing.** Activity simply for activity's sake doesn't usually result in good learning. Debriefing—evaluating an experience by discussing it in pairs or small groups—helps focus the experience and draw out its meaning. Debriefing helps sort and order the information students gather during the experience. It helps learners relate the recently experienced activity to their lives.

The process of debriefing is best started immediately after an experience. We use a three-step process in debriefing: reflection, interpretation, and application.

Reflection—This first step asks the students, "How did you feel?" Active-learning experiences typically evoke an emotional reaction, so it's appropriate to begin debriefing at that level.

Some people ask, "What do feelings have to do with education?" Feelings have everything to do with education. Think back again to that time in your life when you learned a big lesson. In all likelihood, strong feelings accompanied that lesson. Our emotions tend to cement things into our memories.

When you're debriefing, use open-ended questions to probe feelings. Avoid questions that can be answered with a "yes" or "no." Let your learners know that there are no wrong answers to these "feeling" questions. Everyone's feelings are valid.

Interpretation—The next step in the debriefing process asks, "What does this mean to you? How is this experience like or unlike some other aspect of your life?" Now you're asking people to identify a message or principle from the experience.

You want your learners to discover the message for themselves. So instead of telling students your answers, take the time to ask questions that encourage self-discovery. Use Scripture and discussion in pairs or small groups to explore how the actions and effects of the activity might translate to their lives.

Alert! Some of your people may interpret wonderful messages that you never intended. That's not failure! That's the Holy Spirit at work. God allows us to catch different glimpses of his kingdom even when we all look through the same glass.

Application—The final debriefing step asks, "What will you do about it?" This step moves learning into action. Your young people have shared a common experience. They've discovered a principle. Now they must create something new with what they've just experienced and interpreted. They must integrate the message into their lives.

The application stage of debriefing calls for a decision. Ask your students how they'll change, how they'll grow, what they'll do as a result of your time together.

2. Teenagers Need to Think

Today's students have been trained not to think. They aren't dumber than previous generations. We've simply conditioned them not to use their heads.

You see, we've trained our kids to respond with the simplistic answers they think the teacher wants to hear. Fill-in-the-blank student workbooks and teachers who ask dead-end questions such as "What's the capital of Delaware?" have produced kids and adults who have learned not to think.

And it doesn't just happen in junior high or high school. Our children are schooled very early not to think. Teachers attempt to help kids read with nonsensical fill-in-the-blank drills, word scrambles, and missing-letter puzzles.

Helping teenagers think requires a paradigm shift in how we teach. We need to plan for and set aside time for higher-order thinking and be willing to reduce our time spent on lower-order parroting. Group's Core Belief Bible Study Series is designed to help you do just that.

Thinking classrooms look quite different from traditional classrooms. In most church environments, the teacher does most of the talking and hopes that knowledge will transmit from his or her brain to the students'. In thinking settings, the teacher coaches students to ponder, wonder, imagine, and problem-solve.

3. Teenagers Need to Talk

Everyone knows that the person who learns the most in any class is the teacher. Explaining a concept to someone else is usually more helpful to the explainer than to the listener. So why not let the students do more teaching? That's one of the chief benefits of letting kids do the talking. This process is called interactive learning.

What is interactive learning? Interactive learning occurs when students discuss and work cooperatively in pairs or small groups.

Interactive learning encourages learners to work together. It honors the fact that students can learn from one another, not just from the teacher. Students work together in pairs or small groups to accomplish shared goals. They build together, discuss together, and present together. They teach each other and learn from one another. Success as a group is celebrated. Positive interdependence promotes individual and group learning.

Interactive learning not only helps people learn but also helps learners feel better about themselves and get along better with others. It accomplishes these things more effectively than the independent or competitive methods.

Here's a selection of interactive learning techniques that are used in Group's Core Belief Bible Study Series. With any of these models, leaders may assign students to specific partners or small groups. This will maximize cooperation and learning by preventing all the "rowdies" from linking up. And it will allow for new friendships to form outside of established cliques.

Following any period of partner or small-group work, the leader may reconvene the entire class for large-group processing. During this time the teacher may ask for reports or discoveries from individuals or teams. This technique builds in accountability for the teacherless pairs and small groups.

Pair-Share—With this technique each student turns to a partner and responds to a question or problem from the teacher or leader. Every learner responds. There are no passive observers. The teacher may then ask people to share their partners' responses.

Study Partners—Most curricula and most teachers call for Scripture passages to be read to the whole class by one person. One reads; the others doze.

Why not relinquish some teacher control and let partners read and react with each other? They'll all be involved—and will learn more.

Learning Groups—Students work together in small groups to create a model, design artwork, or study a passage or story; then they discuss what they learned through the experience. Each person in the learning group may be assigned a specific role. Here are some examples:

Reader

Recorder (makes notes of key thoughts expressed during the reading or discussion)

Checker (makes sure everyone understands and agrees with answers arrived at by the group)

Encourager (urges silent members to share their thoughts)

When everyone has a specific responsibility, knows what it is, and contributes to a small group, much is accomplished and much is learned.

Summary Partners—One student reads a paragraph, then the partner summarizes the paragraph or interprets its meaning. Partners alternate roles with each paragraph.

The paraphrasing technique also works well in discussions. Anyone who wishes to share a thought must first paraphrase what the previous person said. This sharpens listening skills and demonstrates the power of feedback communication.

Jigsaw—Each person in a small group examines a different concept, Scripture, or part of an issue. Then each teaches the others in the group. Thus, all members teach, and all must learn the others' discoveries. This technique is called a jigsaw because individuals are responsible to their group for different pieces of the puzzle.

JIGSAW EXAMPLE

Here's an example of a jigsaw.

Assign four-person teams. Have teammates each number off from one to four. Have all the Ones go to one corner of the room, all the Twos to another corner, and so on.

Tell team members they're responsible for learning information in their numbered corners and then for teaching their team members when they return to their original teams.

Give the following assignments to various groups:

Ones: Read Psalm 22. Discuss and list the prophecies made about Jesus.

Twos: Read Isaiah 52:13–53:12. Discuss and list the prophecies made about Jesus.

Threes: Read Matthew 27:1-32. Discuss and list the things that happened to Jesus.

Fours: Read Matthew 27:33-66. Discuss and list the things that happened to Jesus.

After the corner groups meet and discuss, instruct all learners to return to their original teams and report what they've learned. Then have each team determine which prophecies about Jesus were fulfilled in the passages from Matthew.

Call on various individuals in each team to report one or two prophecies that were fulfilled.

You Can Do It Too!

All this information may sound revolutionary to you, but it's really not. God has been using active and interactive learning to teach his people for generations. Just look at Abraham and Isaac, Jacob and Esau, Moses and the Israelites, Ruth and Boaz. And then there's Jesus, who used active learning all the time!

Group's Core Belief Bible Study Series makes it easy for you to use active and interactive learning with your group. The active and interactive elements are automatically built in! Just follow the outlines, and watch as your kids grow through experience and positive interaction with others.

FOR DEEPER STUDY

For more information on incorporating active and interactive learning into your work with teenagers, check out these resources:

● *Why Nobody Learns Much of Anything at Church: And How to Fix It,* by Thom and Joani Schultz (Group Publishing) and

● *Do It! Active Learning in Youth Ministry,* by Thom and Joani Schultz (Group Publishing).

your evaluation of core belief

Bible Study Series
for junior high/middle school

the truth about
SIN AND FORGIVENESS

Group Publishing, Inc.
Attention: Core Belief Talk-Back
P.O. Box 481
Loveland, CO 80539
Fax: (970) 669-1994

Please help us continue to provide innovative and useful resources for ministry. After you've led the studies in this volume, take a moment to fill out this evaluation; then mail or fax it to us at the address above. Thanks!

••••••

1. As a whole, this book has been (circle one)

not very helpful   very helpful
1   2   3   4   5   6   7   8   9   10

2. The best things about this book:

3. How this book could be improved:

4. What I will change because of this book:

5. Would you be interested in field-testing future Core Belief Bible Studies and giving us your feedback? If so, please complete the information below:

Name _____

Street address _____

City _____ State _____ Zip _____

Daytime telephone (____) _____ Date _____

THANKS!